N. C. Wyeth

D1393376

a book of postcards

POMEGRANATE ARTBOOKS
SAN FRANCISCO

Pomegranate Artbooks
Box 6099
Rohnert Park, CA 94927

Pomegranate Europe Ltd.
Fullbridge House, Fullbridge
Maldon, Essex CM9 7LE
England

ISBN 0-87654-493-6
Pomegranate Catalog No. A792

Pomegranate publishes books of
postcards on a wide range of subjects.
Please write to the publisher for more information.

Designed by Young Jin Kim
Printed in Korea
05 04 03 02 01 00 99 98 97 96   11 10 9 8 7 6 5 4 3 2

Newell Convers Wyeth (1882–1945), founder of a family dynasty of artists that included his son Andrew and his grandson Jamie, was one of America's preeminent illustrators. N. C. Wyeth's artwork brought to vivid life the lusty characters in such classic books as Robert Louis Stevenson's *Treasure Island, Kidnapped,* and *The Black Arrow* as well as some of the other Scribner's Illustrated Classics: *The Boy's King Arthur, The Last of the Mohicans,* and *The Deerslayer.* His illustrations appeared regularly in the *Saturday Evening Post, Scribner's, Ladies' Home Journal,* and *Collier's Weekly* magazines, the leading periodicals of the day. Wyeth's imaginative genius also found expression in heroic murals for state capitol buildings, banks, and insurance companies and even in altar panels for the National Episcopal Church in Washington, D.C. A highly productive artist, Wyeth produced an enormous volume of work, including more than three thousand known paintings and forty-four enormous murals.

"The genuineness of the artist's work," he insisted, "depends upon the genuineness of the artist's living. In other words, art is not what you do, it is what you are. We cannot in art produce a fraction more than what we are." Wyeth's enthusiasm for life and his lively imagination brought forth a wealth of vibrant images. His youthful experience of farm life — splitting logs, plowing, saddling horses, working with scythes — enabled him to invest his characters with a striking sense of physical authenticity. "After painting action scenes," he commented, "I have ached for hours because of having put myself in the other fellow's shoes as I realized him on canvas." His love of the American spirit and landscape led him to create stunningly realistic historic scenes. His depictions of the old West were garnered from his travels through the region, while his paintings of the Maine seacoast arose from his New England roots; his impressionistic scenes of the countryside originated from his life on the banks of Pennsylvania's Brandywine River. His love of the techniques of the old masters is evident in his work, but Wyeth's unique creative spirit added a powerful sense of mood, period, and place to his paintings and illustrations, investing each with an ambience that makes it immediately recognizable as "an N. C. Wyeth." This book of postcards presents thirty well-loved images from this versatile and prolific American artist. ∎

N. C. Wyeth (American, 1882–1945)
Dark Harbor Fishermen, 1943
Oil on canvas, 47½ x 57½ in.

POMEGRANATE BOX 6099 ROHNERT PARK CA 94927

N. C. Wyeth (AMERICAN, 1882–1945)

Sir Lancelot and Sir Turquine
Oil on canvas, 40 x 32 in.
Illustration for *The Boy's King Arthur*,
edited by Sidney Lanier (New York:
Charles Scribner's Sons, 1917)

POMEGRANATE BOX 6099 ROHNERT PARK CA 94927

N. C. Wyeth (AMERICAN, 1882–1945)

The Deerslayer
Oil on canvas, 40 x 32 in.
Illustration for *The Deerslayer*, by James Fenimore Cooper
(New York: Charles Scribner's Sons, 1925)

POMEGRANATE BOX 6099 ROHNERT PARK CA 94927

N. C. Wyeth (AMERICAN, 1882–1945)

Lesby, 1930
Oil on canvas, 40 x 30 in.
Frontispiece and dustcover for *Lesby*, by Elizabeth Willis
(New York: Charles Scribner's Sons, 1931)

POMEGRANATE BOX 6099 ROHNERT PARK CA 94927

N. C. Wyeth (AMERICAN, 1882–1945)

The Slaughter of the Suitors
Oil on canvas, 48¼ x 38¼ in.
Illustration for *The Odyssey of Homer*, translated by George
Herbert Palmer (Boston: Houghton Mifflin, 1929)

POMEGRANATE BOX 6099 ROHNERT PARK, CA 94927

N. C. Wyeth (AMERICAN, 1882–1945)
Summer, 1909
Oil on canvas, 33½ x 30 in.
Illustration for "The Moods," by George T. Marsh,
Scribner's Magazine, December 1909

POMEGRANATE BOX 6099 ROHNERT PARK CA 94927

From the Archives of the American Illustrators
Gallery, New York City

N. C. Wyeth (American, 1882–1945)
Captain Smollet Defies the Mutineers
Oil on canvas, 47 x 38 in.
Illustration for *Treasure Island*, by Robert Louis Stevenson
(New York: Charles Scribner's Sons, 1911)

Pomegranate Box 6099 Rohnert Park CA 94927

N. C. Wyeth (AMERICAN, 1882–1945)
Snowbound, 1913
Oil on canvas, 36 x 34 in.

POMEGRANATE BOX 6099 ROHNERT PARK CA 94927

From the Archives of the American Illustrators
Gallery, New York City

N. C. Wyeth (AMERICAN, 1882–1945)
The Assassination of Fletcher Christian, 1940
Oil on gessoed panel, 26¼ x 18¼ in.
Illustration for *The Bounty Trilogy—Pitcain's Island*,
by Charles Nordhoff and J. N. Hall (Boston: Little,
Brown, 1940)

POMEGRANATE BOX 6099 ROHNERT PARK CA 94927

N. C. Wyeth (AMERICAN, 1882–1945)
Wallace's Vision, 1921
Oil on canvas, 40 x 32 in.
Illustration for *The Scottish Chiefs*, by Jane Porter
(New York: Charles Scribner's Sons, 1921)

POMEGRANATE BOX 6099 ROHNERT PARK CA 94927

Collection of Sommerville Manning Gallery
From the Archives of the American Illustrators
Gallery, New York City

N. C. Wyeth (AMERICAN, 1882–1945)
Jonathan and David, c. 1929
Oil on canvas, 42 x 32 in.
Illustration for "Children of the Bible," by Bruce Barton,
Good Housekeeping, June 1929

POMEGRANATE   BOX 6099   ROHNERT PARK CA 94927

N. C. Wyeth (AMERICAN, 1882–1945)
Captain George Waymouth on the Georges River
Tempera on panel, 32 x 24½ in.
Frontispiece for *Trending into Maine*,
by Kenneth Roberts (Boston: Little, Brown, 1938)

POMEGRANATE   BOX 6099   ROHNERT PARK CA 94927

From the Archives of the American Illustrators
Gallery, New York City

N. C. Wyeth (AMERICAN, 1882–1945)
The Rakish Brigantine (*Sea Captain in Storm*)
Oil on canvas, 40 x 32 in.
Illustration for *Scribner's Magazine*, August 1914

POMEGRANATE BOX 6099 ROHNERT PARK CA 94927

From the Archives of the American Illustrators
Gallery, New York City

N. C. Wyeth (AMERICAN, 1882–1945)
The Magic Pool, 1906
Oil on canvas, 26 x 38 in.
Illustration for *The Outing Magazine*, June 1907,
The Indian and His Solitude Series, Vol. L, No. 3
Frontispiece for *The Indian in His Solitude*

POMEGRANATE BOX 6099 ROHNERT PARK CA 94927

N. C. Wyeth (Ameriᴄᴀɴ, 1882–1945)
Miss Margy and Bee Man John
Oil on canvas, 40 x 32 in.
Illustration for "The Wild Woman's Lullaby,"
by Constance Skinner, *Scribner's Magazine*, December 1916

Pomegranate Box 6099 Rohnert Park CA 94927

N. C. Wyeth (AMERICAN, 1882–1945)
Alleyne's Ride with a Message for the Prince
Oil on canvas, 40 x 30 in.
Illustration for *The White Company*, by Arthur Conan Doyle
(New York: Cosmopolitan, 1922)

POMEGRANATE BOX 6099 ROHNERT PARK CA 94927

N. C. Wyeth (AMERICAN, 1882–1945)

Drums, 1925
Oil on canvas, 42 x 29 in.
Cover illustration for *Drums*, by James Boyd
(New York: Charles Scribner's Sons, 1925)

POMEGRANATE   BOX 6099   ROHNERT PARK, CA 94927

N. C. Wyeth (AMERICAN, 1882–1945)

Even Unto Bethlehem
Oil on canvas, 52 x 32 in.
Frontispiece and dust jacket for *Even Unto Bethlehem:*
The Story of Christmas, by Henry Van Dyke (New York:
Charles Scribner's Sons, 1928)

POMEGRANATE BOX 6099 ROHNERT PARK CA 94927

N. C. Wyeth (AMERICAN, 1882–1945)
Sir Nigel Sustains England's Honor, 1912
Oil on canvas, 40 x 30 in.
Illustration for *The White Company*, by Arthur Conan Doyle
(New York: Cosmopolitan, 1922)

POMEGRANATE BOX 6099 ROHNERT PARK CA 94927

Collection of Millport Conservancy
From the Archives of the American Illustrators
Gallery, New York City

N. C. Wyeth (AMERICAN, 1882–1945)

Lobsterman Hauling in a Light Fog, 1938
Oil on canvas, 59 x 51½ in.
Illustration for *Trending into Maine*, by Kenneth Roberts
(Boston: Little, Brown, 1938)

POMEGRANATE   BOX 6099   ROHNERT PARK, CA 94927

From the Archives of the American Illustrators
Gallery, New York City

N. C. Wyeth (American, 1882–1945)
Invocation to the Buffalo Herds, 1908
Oil on canvas, 36 x 26 in.

Pomegranate Box 6099 Rohnert Park CA 94927

From the Archives of the American Illustrators
Gallery, New York City

N. C. Wyeth (AMERICAN, 1882–1945)
The Sea Serpent, 1938
Tempera on panel, 33 x 23 in.
Illustration for *Trending into Maine*, by Kenneth Roberts
(Boston: Little, Brown, 1938)

POMEGRANATE BOX 6099 ROHNERT PARK CA 94927

Collection of Millport Conservancy
From the Archives of the American Illustrators
Gallery, New York City

N. C. Wyeth (AMERICAN, 1882–1945)
Old Prospector
Oil on canvas, 36 x 28 in.
Cover illustration for *The Popular Magazine*,
December 15, 1912, Month End Edition

POMEGRANATE   BOX 6099   ROHNERT PARK CA 94927

N. C. Wyeth (AMERICAN, 1882–1945)
In the Tower of London, 1921
Oil on canvas, 40 x 32 in.
Illustration for *The Scottish Chiefs*, by Jane Porter
(New York: Charles Scribner's Sons, 1921)

POMEGRANATE   BOX 6099   ROHNERT PARK, CA 94927

From the Archives of the American Illustrators
Gallery, New York City

N. C. Wyeth (American, 1882–1945)
The Sign and the Heavens, 1918
Oil on canvas, 39½ x 31 in.
Illustration for "The New Crusaders Enter Jerusalem,"
Red Cross magazine, February 1918

Pomegranate Box 6099 Rohnert Park CA 94927

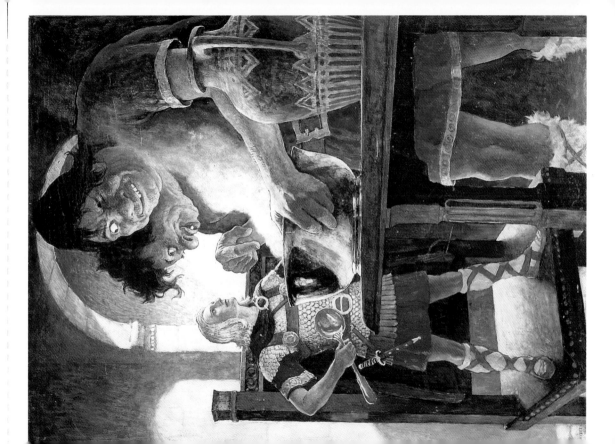

N. C. Wyeth (AMERICAN, 1882–1945)
The Two-Headed Giant
Tempera on plasterboard, 34 x 24 in.
Illustration for *Anthology of Children's Literature*,
compiled by Edna Johnson and Carrie E. Scott
(Cambridge: Riverside Press, 1940)

POMEGRANATE BOX 6099 ROHNERT PARK CA 94927

N. C. Wyeth (AMERICAN, 1882–1945)
A Song of the South, 1925
Oil on canvas, 32 x 30 in.

POMEGRANATE   BOX 6099   ROHNERT PARK, CA 94927

From the Archives of the American Illustrators
Gallery, New York City

N. C. Wyeth (AMERICAN, 1882–1945)

The Lively Lady
Oil on canvas, 23 x 31 in.
Illustration for *The Lively Lady,* by Kenneth Roberts
(New York: Doubleday, Doran, 1931)

POMEGRANATE   BOX 6099   ROHNERT PARK CA 94927

From the Archives of the American Illustrators
Gallery, New York City

N. C. Wyeth (AMERICAN, 1882–1945)

Indian Prayer
Tempera on gessoed panel, 37 x 27 in.
Illustration for *The World of Music: Discovery*, edited by
Mabelle Glenn, Helen S. Leavitt, Victor L. F. Rebmann,
and Earl L. Baker (Boston: Ginn & Co., 1937)

POMEGRANATE   BOX 6099   ROHNERT PARK CA 94927

N. C. Wyeth (AMERICAN, 1882–1945)

Heidi
Oil on canvas, 40 x 32 in.
Illustration for *Anthology of Children's Literature*,
compiled by Edna Johnson and Carrie E. Scott
(Cambridge: Riverside Press, 1940)

POMEGRANATE BOX 6099 ROHNERT PARK CA 94927